Family Photographs

of

Elisha Calkins

&

Anna Dalrymple

Descendants

By **Donovan Hurst**

November 1, 2012

Also Available:

Elisha Calkins & Anna Dalrymple Descendants by Donovan Hurst

Front Cover Image: Calkins Family Photo Album circa 1865

ISBN: 0985696818
ISBN-13: 978-0-9856968-1-8

Dedication

This work is dedicated to all of those that came before us and shaped our lives to make us the people that we are today.

"We are not famous, we are farmers."

Contents

Introduction

This work provides photographs of the family of Mayflower descendant Elisha Calkins & Anna Dalrymple, who settled in the town of Otselic, in the county of Chenango, in the State of New York and their descendants.

Elisha Calkins connection to the ship "Mayflower" is a s follows: Edward Fuller (Passenger on board the ship "Mayflower") married to Unknown, son Samuel Fuller married to Jane Lothrop, son John Fuller married to Mehitable Rowley, daughter Thankful Fuller married to Jabez Crippen, son Thomas Crippen married to Deborah Unknown, daughter Deborah Crippen married Joseph Calkins, and son Elisha Calkins married to Anna Dalrymple, the subject of this work.

All of the photographs presented in this work is believed to be true and accurate based on the research conducted by the author.

For more detailed information regarding each of the individuals found in this work, please refer to the following work, which is currently available for sale:

Elisha Calkins & Anna Dalrymple Descendants by Donovan Hurst

Calkins Family Photo Album

Elisha Tracy Calkins

HART'S. WATERTOWN, N.Y.

Adams, N.Y.

Left (Top): **Dorman Calkins**

Right (Top): **Phebe (Webb) Calkins**

Left (Bottom): **John C. Miller**

Right (Bottom): **Mary Calkins**

Left (Top): **Unknown Girl Tintype-Flipped** Middle (Top): **Almira Calkins** Right (Top): **Lester A. Woods**

Left (Bottom): **Unknown Boy Tintype-Flipped** Right (Bottom): **Leman Calkins Tintype-Flipped**

Left (Top): **Elisha Calkins**   Right (Top): **Anna Dalrymple**

Left (Bottom): **Sarah Ann (Woods) Calkins**   Right (Bottom): **Freeman Calkins**

Left (Top): **Unknown Girl**   Right (Top): **Harriet Calkins**

Left (Bottom): **A. E. Kilby**   Right (Bottom): **Truman D. Calkins**

HART'S,   WATERTOWN, N.Y.

Left (Top): **Unknown Girl**   Right (Top): **Amy Albee Calkins**

Left (Bottom): **William Riley Calkins**   Right (Bottom): **Catharine Maria (Richard) Calkins**

Left (Top): **Ery W. Stokes**   Right (Top): **Philander Butts**

Left (Bottom): **Laura H. Calkins**   Right (Bottom): **Alexander Butts**

Left (Top): **Heman Calkins**   Middle (Top): **Dorman Calkins**

Right (Top): **Unknown Boy Tintype-Flipped**   Left (Bottom): **Louisa Calkins**

Middle (Bottom): **Unknown Child**   Right (Bottom): **Unknown Girl Tintype-Flipped**

Left (Top): **William Riley Calkins**   Right (Top): **Catharine Maria (Richard) Calkins**

Left (Bottom): **Heman Calkins**   Right (Bottom): **Almira (Webb) Calkins**

Left (Top): **Unknown Girl**   Middle (Top): **Unknown Girl**

Left (Bottom): **Samuel Calkins Butts**   Middle (Bottom): **Eliza M. (McMinn) Butts**

Right (Bottom): **Nancy & Ransom Butts**

Left (Top): **Sidney M. Calkins Tintype-Flipped**   Middle (Top): **Lyman Simon Calkins**

Right (Top): **Samuel Calkins Butts Tintype-Flipped**

Left (Bottom): **Elisha Calkins Tintype-Flipped**   Middle (Bottom): **Anna Dalrymple Tintype-Flipped**

Right (Bottom): **Leman & Sidney M. Calkins Tintype-Flipped**

Elisha Calkins & Anna Dalrymple

Left (Top): **Elisha Calkins Tintype-Flipped**   Middle (Top): **Anna Dalrymple Tintype-Flipped**

Right (Top): **Anna Dalrymple photograph of Tintype-Flipped**

Left (Bottom): **Elisha Calkins Ambrotype-Flipped**   Right (Bottom): **Anna Dalrymple Ambrotype-Flipped**

Left & Middle (Top): **Elisha Calkins**   Right (Top): **Anna Dalrymple**

Left (Bottom): **Elisha Calkins**   Middle & Right (Bottom): **Anna Dalrymple**

Left (Top): **Elisha Calkins Ambrotype-Flipped**   Right (Top): **Elisha Calkins Ambrotype-Flipped**

Left (Bottom): **Anna Dalrymple Ambrotype-Flipped**   Right (Bottom): **Anna Dalrymple**

Truman D. Calkins & Abigail P. Rogers Miles Family

G. F. LEWIS, Carthage. N. Y.

Left (Top): **Truman D. Calkins Ambrotype-Flipped**   Right (Top): **Truman D. Calkins**

Left (Bottom): **Truman D. Calkins**   Right (Bottom): **Truman D. Calkins**

Left (Top): **Elisha Tracy Calkins**   Right (Top): **Elisha Tracy Calkins**

Left (Bottom): **Celinda C. Ray**   Right (Bottom): **Celinda C. Ray 1888**

Left (Top): **Alice B. (Calkins) Stowell**   Right (Top): **Clinton H. Stowell**

Left (Bottom): **George LaFayette Stowell**   Right (Bottom): **George LaFayette Stowell**

MADISON. De Witt. NEW YORK.

DUPLICATES FURNISHED.

Minnie L. Calkins

Left: **Daughters of Truman D. Calkins**   Right: **Daughters of Truman D. Calkins**

Left: **Rowena Calkins**   Right: **Charlotte Melissa Calkins**

Left (Top): **Lydia Ann Calkins** Right (Top): **Lydia Ann (Calkins) Walradt 1893**

Middle (Bottom): **Walradt or Walrod Family 1887**

Left (Top): **Lydia Ann (Calkins) Walradt or Walrod**   Right (Top): **Jacob Walradt or Walrod**

Left (Bottom): **Abigail Delina Walradt or Walrod**   Right (Bottom): **Irving Jacob Walradt or Walrod**

Left (Top): **Unknown Girl Walradt**   Right (Top): **Unknown Girl Walradt**

Left (Bottom): **Unknown Walradt Children**   Right (Bottom): **Unknown Baby Walradt**

Left (Top): **Weaver Wilson Calkins 1888**   Right (Top): **Weaver Wilson Calkins**

Left (Bottom): **Melissa (Young) Calkins**   Right (Bottom): **Adella Calkins**

Mary Calkins & John C. Miller Family

Left: **Mary Calkins**   Right: **John C. Miller**

Laura H. Calkins & Alexander Butts Family

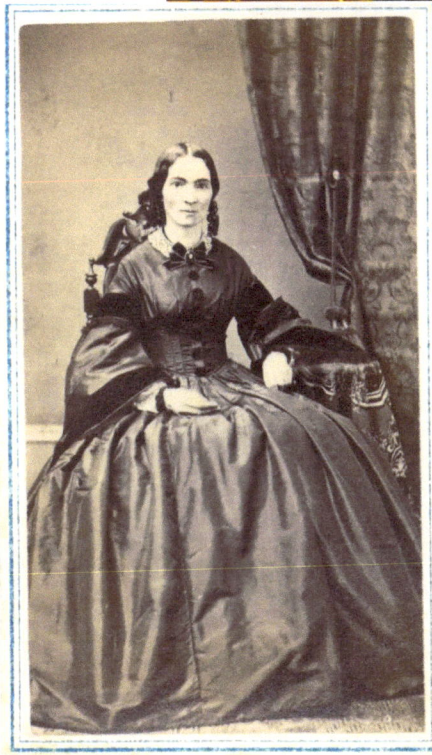

Top (Middle): **Laura H. Calkins Ambrotype-Flipped**

Left (Bottom): **Laura H. Calkins**   Right (Bottom): **Alexander Butts & Laura H. Calkins**

Left: **Laura H. Calkins**   Right: **Alexander Butts**

Left (Top): **Samuel Calkins Butts Ambrotype-Flipped**

Right (Top) & Left (Bottom): **Samuel Calkins Butts Tintype-Flipped**

Middle (Bottom): **Eliza M. (McMinn) Butts**   Right (Bottom): **Nancy & Ransom Butts**

Almira Calkins & Lester A. Woods Family

Middle (Top): **Almira Calkins Tintype-Flipped**

Left (Bottom): **Almira Calkins Ambrotype-Flipped**

Right (Bottom): **Lester A. Woods & Almira Calkins Ambrotype-Flipped**

Left (Top): **Almira (Calkins) Woods** Right (Top): **Lester A. Woods**

Left (Bottom): **Almira (Calkins) Woods** Right (Bottom): **Lester A. Woods**

Freeman Calkins & Sarah Ann Woods Family

Left (Top & Middle): **Freeman Calkins**   Right (Top): **Sarah Ann (Woods) Calkins**

Left & Right (Bottom): **Freeman Calkins Ambrotype-Flipped**

Left & Middle (Top): **Freeman Calkins**   Right (Top): **Sarah Ann (Woods) Calkins March 1865**

Left & Middle (Bottom): **Freeman & Sarah Ann (Woods) Calkins**

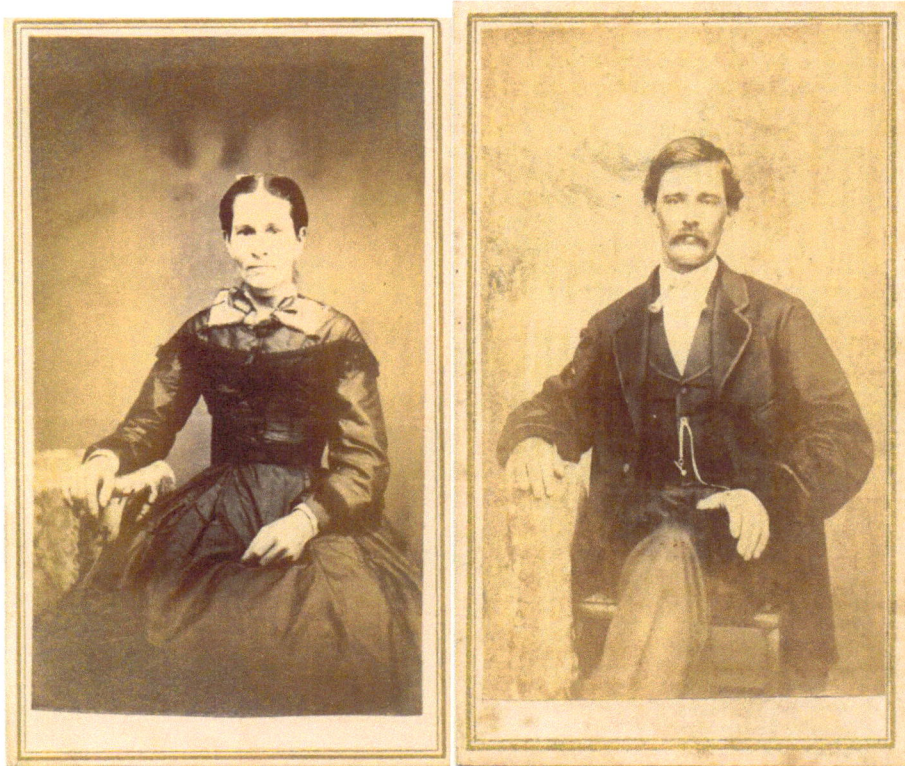

Top (Middle): **Sarah Ann (Woods) Calkins**

Left (Top): **Fidelia Lossie Calkins**   Right (Top): **William Riley Calkins**

Left (Top): **Fidelia Lossie (Calkins) Fuller**   Right (Top): **Carlton Washington Fuller**

Left (Bottom): **Frederick Deforest Fuller**   Right (Bottom): **Frank Alvah Fuller**

Left (Top): **William Riley Calkins**   Right (Top): **William Riley Calkins**

Left (Bottom): **William Riley Calkins**   Right (Bottom): **Mary Etta Perry**

William Riley Calkins holding William Arthur Calkins &

Mary Etta (Perry) Calkins holding Mabel Effie Calkins – Circa 1892

Left (Top): **Lora Deloss Calkins & Eva Estella Dickinson**

Right (Top): **Delbert C. Calkins & Maud P. Brott**

Left (Bottom): **Clara May Calkins**   Right (Bottom): **Llwellyn Elwin Claflin & Clara May Calkins**

Left (Top): **James Werdna Calkins** Right (Top): **James Werdna Calkins & Alice Nettie Richardson**

Left (Bottom): **Floyd Elisha Calkins & Minnie Thompson** Right (Bottom): **Minnie Thompson**

Left: **William Arthur Calkins & Sadie Anita Cecelia Nelson**

Right: **Mabel Effie Calkins & George Leland Morgan**

Lyman Simon Calkins & Amy Albee Family

Left (Top): **Lyman Simon Calkins Ambrotype-Flipped**   Right (Top): **Amy Albee Ambrotype-Flipped**

Left (Bottom): **Lyman Simon Calkins**   Right (Bottom): **Amy (Albee) Calkins**

N. O. CALKINS.

Left (Top): **Lyman Simon Calkins Tintype-Flipped**

Middle: **Lyman Simon and Amy (Albee) Calkins**   Right (Top): **Amy (Albee) Calkins**

Left (Bottom): **Arcus Riley Calkins**   Right (Bottom): **Nathan Orson Calkins**

Heman Calkins & Almira Webb Family

Left (Top): **Heman Calkins Tintype-Flipped**   Right (Top): **Heman Calkins Ambrotype-Flipped**

Left (Bottom): **Heman Calkins Ambrotrype-Flipped**   Right (Bottom): **Heman Calkins**

Left (Top): **Heman Calkins**   Right (Top): **Almira (Webb) Calkins**

Left (Bottom): **Heman Calkins**   Right (Bottom): **Almira (Webb) Calkins**

Left: **Sidney M. Calkins**   Right: **Sidney M. Calkins**

Left (Top): **Leman Calkins**   Right (Top): **Louisa Bellinger**

Middle (Bottom): **James H. Calkins**

Left (Top): **Louisa (Calkins) Rider 1889**   Right (Top): **Daniel B. Rider 1891**

Middle (Bottom): **Charles A. Rider 1889**

Left (Top): **William Henry Calkins Tintype-Flipped**   Right (Top): **William Henry Calkins**

Middle (Bottom): **Sally Ann Calkins 1891**

Left (Top): **Morrell Calkins**   Right (Top): **Morrell Calkins**

Middle (Bottom): **Morrell Calkins 1887**

Dorman Calkins & Phebe Webb Family

Left (Top): **Dorman Calkins Ambrotype-Flipped**   Right (Top): **Dorman Calkins Ambrotype-Flipped**

Middle (Bottom): **Dorman Calkins Ambrotype-Flipped**

Middle (Top): **Dorman Calkins**

Left (Bottom): **Dorman Calkins Tintype-Flipped**   Right (Bottom): **Dorman Calkins**

Left (Top): **Dorman Calkins**   Right (Top): **Phebe (Webb) Calkins**

Left (Bottom): **Dorman Calkins**   Right (Bottom): **Phebe (Webb) Calkins 1884**

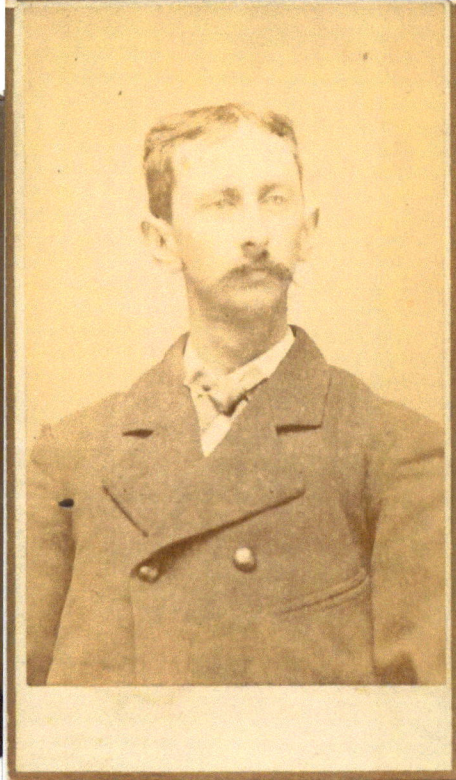

Left (Top): **Peruda Calkins Tintype-Flipped**   Right (Top): **Peruda Calkins 1887**

Left (Bottom): **Dorman Dwight Calkins Tintype-Flipped**   Right (Bottom): **Dorman Dwight Calkins**

Harriet Calkins & Ery W. Stokes Family

Left (Top): **Harriet Calkins**   Right (Top): **Harriet (Calkins) Stokes 1887**

Left (Bottom): **Ery W. Stokes Ambrotype-Flipped**   Right (Bottom): **Ery W. Stokes**

Left (Top): **Child of Harriet Calkins Ambrotype-Flipped**   Right (Top): **Olivia L. Stokes 1888**

Left (Bottom): **Ida E. (Stokes) Shepardson 1893**   Right (Bottom): **Walter A. Shepardson 1912**

William Riley Calkins & Catharine Maria Richard Family

Left (Top) & Right (Top): **William Riley Calkins Ambrotype-Flipped**

Middle (Bottom): **Catharine Maria (Richard) Calkins & William Riley Calkins Ambrotype-Flipped**

Left (Top): **William Riley Calkins**   Right (Top): **Catharine Maria (Richard) Calkins**

Left (Bottom): **William Riley Calkins**   Right (Bottom): **Catharine Maria (Richard) Calkins**

Left (Top): **William Riley Calkins 1891**   Right (Top): **Tyler Wade Calkins 1888**

Left (Bottom): **Tyler Wade Calkins**   Right (Bottom): **Tyler Wade Calkins**

Groups

1st Row (Front): **Lyman Simon Calkins & Mary Calkins**

2nd Row: **Heman Calkins, Laura H. Calkins & Dorman Calkins**

3rd Row: **Almira Calkins, Harriet Calkins & Possibly Sarah Ann Woods**

4th Row (Back): **Truman D. Calkins & Freeman Calkins**

Front: **Catharine Maria Richard, Almira Webb & Phebe Webb**

Back: **William Riley Calkins, Heman Calkins & Dorman Calkins**

Calkins Children Graduation 1891

Previous Page

Front: **Catharine Maria (Richard) Calkins, Laura H. Calkins, Almira Calkins, Truman D. Calkins,**

Mary Calkins & Harriet Calkins

Back: **William Riley Calkins, Freeman Calkins, Dorman Calkins, Heman Calkins &**

Lyman Simon Calkins

October 1, 1873

Next Page

Calkins Family Reunion

Otselic, Chenango Co., New York

October 1, 1873

Index

D

F

K

M

N

P

R

S

T

U

ABOUT THE AUTHOR

Donovan Hurst graduated from San Diego State University with a Bachelor of Arts in the major field of studies of History and a minor in the field of studies of Anthropology. He is a current member of The General Society of Mayflower Descendants and has been conducting genealogical research for over 10 years tracing back his ancestors to their ancestral homelands in Denmark, England, France, Germany, Ireland, Norway, and Scotland.

www.ingramcontent.com/pod-product-compliance
Lightning Source LLC
Chambersburg PA
CBHW060809270326
41928CB00002B/35